Hamlyn Gardening Guide

HOUSE PLANT CARE

Alan Toogood

HAMLYN

ACKNOWLEDGEMENTS
Colour photographs
Pat Brindley, p. 4; Photos Horticultural, p. 9;
The Harry Smith Horticultural Photographic
Collection, p. 7, 10, 12.
All other photographs by Rob Herwig.

Published in 1986 by
Hamlyn Publishing,
Bridge House, London Road,
Twickenham, Middlesex, England

ISBN 0 600 30722 0

Filmset in 9½pt on 11½pt Palatino
by Page Bros (Norwich) Ltd, England

Printed and bound in Italy

CONTENTS

INTRODUCTION

*P*robably never before – except perhaps during the Victorian era – have house plants been more popular than they are today. There is scarcely a home, office, hotel or restaurant that does not have at least a few indoor plants.

And certainly never before have we had such a vast range of plants to choose from, both flowering and foliage kinds. There are plants suitable for every room in the house, from unheated or cool rooms, to very warm rooms with dry air. And there are plants suited to virtually every position in a room, from a dark corner to a sunny windowsill.

There are plants which tolerate a good deal of neglect – ideal, perhaps, for busy business people who may spend a lot of time away from home, or for offices which are often unoccupied during the weekends. There are many easy-going plants which need only a little more care and attention; and if you have plenty of time to devote to plants, and can provide the right

conditions, there are some really choice and flamboyant kinds which will add a truly exotic touch to your home.

Cultivation

Buying plants
House plants can be bought from garden centres, florists and from some chain stores in the high street. There are also a few specialist growers who offer a mail-order service. They generally advertise in the gardening press.

A lot of people buy plants on impulse – and who can blame them, for many are so tempting. However, it is sensible to ensure that you can provide the right conditions for them, in respect of temperature, light and atmospheric humidity, or they may not survive. Also, find out how much care and attention a plant needs before you buy. Generally house plants have pictorial labels which indicate cultural requirements.

As with anything you buy, make

sure the quality is good by thoroughly inspecting the plants. Incidentally, never buy house plants from an open market stall, or those displayed on the pavement outside, say, a greengrocer's shop. Many house plants come from the tropics and will suffer if placed out of doors. When you get them home they may drop their leaves or even die.

Indeed, when you buy a plant from a garden centre, florist or chain store you should ensure it is well wrapped before you take it outside.

How do you recognise quality? Plants should be generally strong and sturdy and the leaves should look in the peak of health. Avoid plants whose leaves are wilting, damaged, have brown edges or brown spots or other marks. Ensure there are no insect pests or diseases on the plants.

Flowering house plants should have plenty of buds, and a few flowers fully open.

Make sure the plants are neither loose in their pots, nor appear too big for their pots. Make sure, too, the soil or compost is moist.

Some plants, particularly flowering kinds, need to be bought at the right season. For instance, there are lots to choose from in the winter, like the winter-flowering begonias, cyclamen, the winter-flowering heath or *Erica gracilis*, the poinsettia or *Euphorbia pulcherrima*, *Primula obconica*, and azaleas or *Rhododendron simsii*. In the spring primulas will still be available, plus cinerarias, calceolarias, *Clivia*

miniata, Cytisus × racemosus, and others. In summer there will be bougainvilleas, pot chrysanthemums (actually available all year round), *Exacum affine*, hibiscus, hydrangea, impatiens, African violets and streptocarpus. In autumn some of these are still available, and also the winter-flowering plants will be coming in.

Displaying plants
No matter how attractive a plant may be, it will do little to enhance a room if it is not displayed or positioned to best advantage. In fact, most of the small house plants look better if arranged in groups. Large specimens, however, especially those with distinctive habits of growth, such as *Monstera deliciosa*, some of the large philodendrons, rubber plants, figs and yuccas, look good in isolation – as specimen plants which act as focal points.

Groups of plants generally consist mainly of foliage kinds, with a few flowering pot plants in season to provide 'splashes' of colour. It is important to ensure that all plants in any one group have the same requirements in respect of temperature, light and humidity.

Plants can be arranged in troughs, say on a windowsill, or in various large containers or 'planters'. There is quite a range available in garden centres.

For those plants which need humid or moist air around them, fill the containers with peat and sink the pots in this up to their rims. The peat should be kept moist to provide humid air.

If you are arranging plants in a windowsill trough, then place a tall plant or two in the centre and grade down to shorter plants towards the ends, to give a triangular shape. Alternatively group tall plants at one end and grade down to short ones at the other. Don't forget to include a few trailing plants at the edges, or at the ends, like ivies and asparagus.

If you want a free-standing group, say in a planter on the floor, then go for a pyramid shape by placing tall plants in the centre and

An attractive arrangement of foliage plants in a trough screens a bare fireplace no longer in use

Plants requiring moist air benefit from being plunged in a container of peat kept permanently damp

light from a window shines through the leaves.

Ornamental pot holders can be used for single plants to hide the plastic pot which is not particularly attractive. Plain colours are recommended as they do not detract from the beauty of the plants.

A novel and very attractive way of displaying some plants, particularly trailing kinds, is to fix some indoor trellis panels (the plastic-coated steel type) to a wall, and to arrrange plastic pot holders on it with special brackets. Plants are then simply placed in the holders.

Trailing plants can also be grown in hanging baskets and hanging pot holders. If you choose baskets,

grading down to shorter ones, and trailing kinds, towards the edges.

When arranging plants in groups try to create contrasts in foliage shape and colour. For instance, try grouping plants with sword-shaped leaves with those which have rounded or hand-shaped leaves. Combine variegated plants with plain green ones.

If they are to show up well house plants need suitable backgrounds. Most would be 'lost' against a background of heavily patterned wallpaper, so try, if possible, to give them a plain background. Mirrors, or mirror tiles, also make good backgrounds, giving the illusion of twice as many plants. Some plants, especially those with paper-thin foliage, are enhanced if

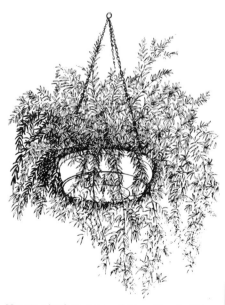

Hanging baskets are available with a built-in drip tray. These are particularly convenient for indoor use

go for the solid plastic type with a built-in drip tray.

The air plants, or epiphytic tillandsias (which grow on trees in the wild) are becoming very popular, and the best way to display these is to gently tie them on to pieces of tree branch or drift wood and hang them up – they could be supported on wall trellis (see opposite).

Light and shade

House plants vary enormously in their light requirements, but it is important to ensure the right conditions for healthy growth. Light requirements are given for each of the plants described in the A to Z of House Plants (page 17).

In general terms, few house plants should be subjected to direct sun, shining through the windows, for it scorches the foliage, except perhaps during the winter when the sun is weak.

Nevertheless, some plants do need very bright light and are therefore best on a south or west facing windowsill, but they could be protected from direct sun with net curtains. These will give bright but diffused light. Most of the flowering house plants, including bulbs, cacti and succulents, need bright light. Actually, cacti are among the few plants that can take direct strong sunshine.

You will find that many house plants, mainly foliage kinds, will thrive in poorer light conditions

This copper kettle provides a novel container for *Fittonia verschaffeltii*, the mosaic plant

further in a room. These are mainly plain green-leaved kinds which originate from the rain forests of the tropics, where conditions are often very gloomy. Again I would refer you to the A to Z of House Plants.

Temperature

To grow house plants successfully you must provide suitable temperatures. Really it is a case of choosing plants to suit the temperature of each room. For

Ferns and other foliage plants enjoy the warm and steamy atmosphere found in a bathroom

instance, if you have an unheated or very cool room, then choose plants which are hardy, or almost hardy, like the ivies, *Fatsia japonica*, × *Fatshedera lizei, Campanula isophylla*, pot chrysanthemums, cyclamen, hydrangeas and primulas.

Many of our house plants, particularly the foliage kinds, come from the tropics, and need fairly high temperatures all year round. They are suited to warm living rooms and the like where the temperature does not drop below 15.5°C (60°F), or certainly not below 13°C (55°F).

Generally speaking, house plants like a steady temperature – in other words, conditions which do not wildly fluctuate.

The problem, though, with warm rooms is that often the air is dry, especially if the house has central heating. Dry air is not suitable for many plants, although some, such as the cacti and succulents, relish it. So some provision will have to be made for humid conditions around plants in a centrally heated room (see section on Humidity, below).

However, do not forget the bathroom and kitchen – in many homes these are quite warm rooms and the atmosphere more humid than in other rooms: ideal conditions for many house plants, particularly the more tricky kinds like African violets, fittonias and caladiums.

Never place plants near a heater or radiators, where the leaves may become badly scorched or simply dry up. Avoid placing them immediately above a heater or radiators.

Another method of keeping up the humidity is to mist house plants over with water at least once a day when the central heating is on

Humidity

We have already touched on the subject of humidity – or moist air around plants. The majority of our house plants do need moist air otherwise the leaves may dry up and shrivel, or turn brown at the edges, and growth generally will be poor. Some plants, though, like dry air – the cacti and succulents, for example, and pelargoniums.

The higher the temperature the more humidity needed. At the other extreme, plants in cool or cold rooms will be better in a dry atmosphere.

How do we provide humidity? One method (plunging pots to their rims in peat, which is kept moist) has been suggested under the section dealing with displaying plants. The alternative is to mist spray the leaves daily in warm conditions, using an indoor hand sprayer. However, plants with hairy or woolly leaves should not be sprayed.

Plants which need warm conditions and very high humidity, like fittonias and African violets, would be better planted in a glass fish tank complete with cover and

Much simpler than a bottle garden is to grow plants in a fish tank. Covering the soil surface with pebbles looks ornamental and helps retain soil moisture

built-in fluorescent tube. Then they will have all the humidity they need without making your room resemble a tropical rain forest! (I would not recommend 'bottle gardens' using a carboy or similar large bottle, for these are difficult to plant and maintain).

Watering

This probably causes more problems than any other aspect of house-plant care. Many people are too kind to their plants, and keep them far too wet, with the result that the roots rot and the plants die. Very often plants are given 'a splash of water' daily, with the result that the compost or soil is permanently wet; or excess water which drains through the pot may collect in the bottom of a pot holder or trough, so the pot is actually standing in water, which saturates the compost.

Bear in mind that plants will need watering more often in warm conditions than in a cool atmosphere, because the compost will dry out more quickly. Plants also need more water in the growing period (spring and summer), for they are using more water. In the autumn and winter, when they are resting, they need far less.

So how do we know when a plant needs watering? It is a case of testing the compost, by pushing a finger down into it, to a depth of about 2.5 cm (1 in). If the compost feels dry, then water is needed. If it is moist or wet, then do not apply water. In the growing season you can, however, safely apply water if the compost is moist just below the surface; but in the winter certainly wait until it has become dry to a depth of 2.5 cm (1 in) or so.

If you do not want to rely on your own judgement, then use one of the proprietary soil moisture meters – the type with a metal probe which is pushed down into the compost. There is a calibrated dial, which indicates 'dry', 'moist' and 'wet'.

Do not forget to use soft or rain water only for those plants which dislike lime – particularly rhododendrons or azaleas.

Feeding
Most house plants benefit from regular feeding in the growing period – approximately from April to September. Fortnightly liquid feeds can be given, using a proprietary house plant fertiliser according to the maker's instructions. If you are inclined to forget to feed your plants, try using fertiliser tablets, which are simply pressed into the compost, when they will steadily release plant foods over a period of several weeks. Don't forget that cacti and succulents also need feeding regularly, contrary to popular belief.

Potting on
For the first few years of their lives most house plants will need potting on each year, in the spring, into larger pots, to give them room to grow, until eventually they are in final-size pots.

Very vigorous plants can be potted on two sizes – for example, from a 10 cm (4 in) to a 15 cm (6 in) pot. Less-vigorous plants are best moved on to the next size of pot.

As a general rule, most small plants will be happy in a final pot size of 15 cm (6 in). Those of slightly more vigorous habit may need 20 cm (8 in) pots, while very large plants, such as the rubber plants and philodendrons, could eventually be given 30 cm (12 in) pots.

If you do not pot on plants they will eventually become potbound, when the compost is packed with roots. Growth will then slow down considerably and may even stop.

Plastic or clay pots can be used. The latter are perhaps better for plants which need really well-drained conditions, such as cacti and succulents, and for very large or tall plants to give them more stability. When using pots of 15 cm (6 in) and over, a layer of drainage

Before planting up large plots, put in a layer of crocks or pebbles covered with some rough peat to ensure good drainage

material should first be placed in the bottom, such as a 2.5 cm (1 in) layer of broken clay flower pots, or shingle. Top this with a thin layer of rough peat.

Before you pot on a plant you should check the root system to find out whether or not the plant really needs to be moved on. To remove a plant from its pot, invert it, tap the rim of the pot on the edge of a table or bench to loosen the rootball, and slide off the pot. If the compost is fully permeated with roots then the plant needs a larger pot. If, however, there is a lot of compost without roots, then it's best leave the plant in its present pot.

When potting on use a slightly larger pot than before (**1**); then after putting some compost in the bottom, trickle compost around the rootball, firming as you go (**2**, **3**)

Potting on is straightforward enough. Place some compost in the bottom of the new pot, set the plant centrally, and trickle compost between the rootball and the side of the pot and firm it with your fingers. After potting, the top of the rootball should be covered with about 1 cm ($\frac{1}{2}$ in) of new compost, and there should be space of between 1 and 2.5 cm ($\frac{1}{2}$ and 1 in) between the compost surface and the rim of the pot (depending on pot size) to allow room for watering.

Plants in final pots can be re-potted every two years or so to provide them with fresh compost. This is done in the spring. Remove the plant from its pot and tease away some of the old compost. A few roots can be cut back if desired. Then put the plant back in the

same pot, filling in with fresh compost.

One has a choice of proprietary peat-based house-plant composts, or traditional soil-based John Innes potting composts. Plants which like well-drained or dryish conditions, like cacti, are better in John Innes. Use J.I. No. 2 for potting on, and No. 1 for potting up rooted cuttings. If you are potting lime-hating plants, such as rhododendrons, use an acid or lime-free compost.

Pests and diseases

The following are the major troubles that are likely to appear. Plants should be sprayed as soon as pests are seen, with a proprietary house-plant insecticide – most come in aerosol form. Any diseases can be controlled by spraying with benomyl fungicide.

Aphids Small plant bugs, green or black, found on tips of shoots and young leaves. They suck the sap and cause distorted growth.

Mealy bugs Like large aphids but covered in a white mealy substance. Found on woody plants, and on cacti and succulents. They cause the same damage as aphids.

Red spider mites These are almost microscopic, and under a hand lens look like little red spiders. They suck sap from the leaves, which results in very fine, pale mottling.

Scale insects These look like brown or greyish scales on the stems of woody plants, and they do not move around. They suck the sap, which weakens the plants.

Whitefly These are small white flies which congregate on the undersides of the leaves of many plants, where they again suck sap.

Grey mould This is a fungal disease which can attack most plants. A grey mould develops on leaves, flowers or stems, which is followed by rotting. Affected parts of plants should be cut away.

Mildew Another fungal disease, this time appearing as powdery white patches on leaves and tips of shoots. Begonias are particularly prone to mildew.

Increasing Plants

Stem cuttings

Plants which produce plenty of new side shoots each year can be propagated from these. In the spring or summer, as soon as shoots are 5 to 7.5 cm (2 to 3 in) long, remove some with a sharp knife. The base of each cutting must be cut cleanly immediately below a leaf joint or node. The leaves should be removed from the lower half. Then dip the base of each cutting in a hormone rooting powder to speed rooting.

Cuttings are inserted firmly up to their lower leaves in a cutting compost – this is mixed at home and consists of equal parts by volume of peat and coarse or sharp sand (never builders' sand). Use pots for cuttings, and water them in after insertion. Heat is needed for rooting, so either place the cuttings in an electrically heated windowsill propagating case; or enclose the entire pot in a clear polythene bag

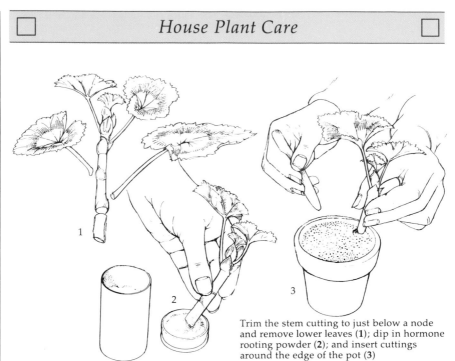

Trim the stem cutting to just below a node and remove lower leaves (**1**); dip in hormone rooting powder (**2**); and insert cuttings around the edge of the pot (**3**)

and place on a windowsill in a warm room. Ventilate this several times a week. When rooted (within about six weeks for most) lift the cuttings and pot into 8 cm (3 in) pots.

Division

Clump-forming plants, like chlorophytums, aspidistras, many ferns, and aglaonemas, can be increased by division in the spring. This simply involves removing the plant from its pot, teasing away much of the compost, and pulling the plant apart into a number of pieces, each complete with roots and top growth. These divisions are then potted into pots of suitable size.

A TO Z
OF
HOUSE PLANTS

Achimenes hybrid Hot-water plant
Habit: perennial plants which grow from
rhizomes and flower in summer and autumn.
Conditions: bright light, any warm room,
humid air. **Care:** plant rhizomes early spring;
dry off after flowering and store.

Adiantum raddianum Maidenhair fern
Habit: a perennial fern about 45 cm (18 in)
high. **Conditions:** bright light, minimum
temperature 15.5°C (60°F), high humidity.
Care: keep steadily moist all year round.
Propagation: by division in spring.

Aechmea fasciata Urn plant
Habit: about 45 cm (18 in) high; long-lasting
flower head. **Conditions:** bright light,
minimum temperature of 10°C (50°F), high
humidity. **Care:** moderate watering, keep
'vase' filled with fresh water.

Aeonium arboreum
Habit: a shrubby succulent plant up to 1 m
(3 ft) high. **Conditions:** bright light, including
some sun, dry air, minimum temperature of
7°C (45°F). **Care:** water moderately and feed
in summer. **Propagation:** stem cuttings.

Agave americana 'Marginata' Century plant
Habit: a wide-spreading succulent plant with
spine-edged leaves. **Conditions:** maximum
light, plus some sun; dry air, minimum
temperature of 10°C (50°F). **Care:** keep dry in
autumn and winter. Use well-drained
compost.

***Aglaonema commutatum
'Pseudobracteatum'*** Chinese evergreen
Habit: a tufted evergreen perennial of dwarf
habit. **Conditions:** minimum temperature of
13°C (55°F); shady conditions; high humidity.
Care: water well, but reduce in winter.
Propagation: division in spring.

Aglaonema treubii 'Silver King' Chinese
evergreen
Habit: a dwarf, tufted evergreen perennial.
Conditions: minimum temperature of 13°C
(55°F); shady conditions; high humidity.
Care: water well, but reduce in winter.
Propagation: divide the plant in spring.

Aloe variegata Partridge-breasted aloe
Habit: a dwarf succulent plant.
Conditions: high temperatures spring and
summer; cool in winter; dry air; full sun.
Care: keep dry in autumn and winter when
resting. **Propagation:** use leaves as cuttings.

Amaryllis belladonna Belladonna lily
Habit: an autumn-flowering bulb.
Conditions: ideal for a cool, light, sunny
porch or sunroom; dry atmosphere. **Care:** pot
bulb in summer, in well-drained compost.
Keep dry when leaves die down.

Ananas comosus 'Variegatus' Variegated
pineapple
Habit: evergreen perennial, forming a wide
spreading rosette. **Conditions:** minimum
temperature of 10°C (50°F); very high
humidity; bright light. **Care:** moderate
watering, reducing still further in winter.

Anthurium scherzerianum Flamingo flower
Habit: evergreen perennial, summer
flowering. **Conditions:** bright light;
minimum temperature of 15.5°C (60°F); very
high humidity. **Care:** water freely in
summer. **Propagation:** division in early
spring.

Aphelandra squarrosa 'Louisae'. Zebra plant
Habit: shrubby evergreen, with long-lasting
flowers. **Conditions:** ideal temperature
around 21°C (70°F); very high humidity; good
light. **Care:** water well, moderately in winter.
Propagation: stem cuttings, spring.

Aporocactus flagelliformis Rat's tail cactus
Habit: flowers freely in spring on long thin
stems. **Conditions:** cool in autumn/winter,
warm for rest of year; full sun and dry air.
Care: keep dry in autumn and winter.
Propagation: cuttings in summer.

Araucaria heterophylla Norfolk Island pine
Habit: evergreen tree, attaining about 2 m
(6 ft) in height. **Conditions:** minimum
temperature of 7°C (45°F), ideally around
15.5°C (60°F); ideal for light shade; humid
atmosphere. Keep only just moist in winter.

Ardisia crispa Coral berry
Habit: shrub of slow growth, berries in
winter. **Conditions:** cool, minimum
temperature 7°C (45°F); bright light, humidity
in warm conditions. **Care:** keep steadily
moist. **Propagation:** stem cuttings in
summer.

Asparagus densiflorus 'Meyeri'
Asparagus fern
Habit: not a true fern, but evergreen
perennial. **Conditions:** minimum
temperature of 13°C (55°F); high humidity;
moderate shade. **Care:** water well, keep moist
in winter. **Propagation:** spring division.

Asparagus densiflorus 'Sprengeri'
Asparagus fern
Habit: useful evergreen trailing perennial.
Conditions: minimum temperature of 13°C
(55°F); high humidity; moderate shade.
Care: water well, but keep slightly moist in
winter. **Propagation:** spring division.

Asparagus setaceus (A. plumosus)
Asparagus fern
Habit: a climbing evergreen perennial.
Conditions: minimum temperature of 7–10°C
(45–50°F); high humidity; light shade.
Care: water well when growing, be sparing
in autumn and winter. **Propagation:** division.

Aspidistra elatior Cast-iron plant
Habit: popular evergreen perennial.
Conditions: tolerates neglect; minimum
temperature 10°C (50°F); moderate humidity;
takes heavy shade. **Care:** water well in
growing season, very sparingly in winter.
Propagation: division.

Aspidistra elatior 'Variegata' Variegated
cast-iron plant
Habit: more striking than the species.
Conditions: temperature and humidity as for
species; provide bright light for best colour.
Care: as for species, but do not overfeed or
colour may fade.

Asplenium bulbiferum Mother fern
Habit: dwarf evergreen fern with plantlets on leaves. **Conditions:** temperature not below 13°C (55°F); low to moderate humidity; good light or light shade. **Care:** keep steadily moist. **Propagation:** pot up plantlets.

Asplenium nidus Bird's nest fern
Habit: slow-growing evergreen fern of modest stature. **Conditions:** reasonably bright light; high humidity; minimum temperature of 15.5°C (60°F). **Care:** keep moist at all times, but not excessively wet.

Begonia boweri Eyelash begonia
Habit: a dwarf begonia with evergreen foliage. **Conditions:** needs warm room, temperature not below 10°C (50°F); very high humidity; good light or slight shade. **Care:** water only when becoming dry. **Propagation:** division.

Begonia corallina Angel-wing begonia
Habit: perennial up to 1.2 m (4 ft) high, flowers in summer. **Conditions:** warm room, not below 10°C (50°F); high humidity; bright light. **Care:** water only when becoming dry. **Propagation:** cuttings in summer.

Begonia elatior hybrid Winter-flowering begonia
Habit: a dwarf tuberous begonia blooming profusely in winter. **Conditions:** ideal temperature 15.5°C (60°F), not below 13°C (55°F); moderate humidity; bright light. **Care:** water only when becoming dry. **Propagation:** cuttings.

Begonia Lorraine hybrid Winter-flowering begonia
Habit: a low-growing begonia which blooms in winter. **Conditions:** ideal temperature 15.5°C (60°F), not below 13°C (55°F); moderate humidity; bright light. **Care:** water only when becoming dry. **Propagation:** cuttings in summer.

Begonia masoniana Iron cross begonia
Habit: a dwarf evergreen foliage begonia. **Conditions:** needs warm room, temperature not below 10°C (50°F); very high humidity; good light or light shade. **Care:** water only when becoming dry. **Propagation:** division.

Begonia rex Rex begonia
Habit: a popular dwarf foliage begonia in various leaf colours. **Conditions:** warm room, not below 10°C (50°F); very high humidity; good light to slight shade. **Care:** water only when becoming dry. **Propagation:** division.

Begonia semperflorens Wax begonia
Habit: a very dwarf begonia generally treated as an annual. **Conditions:** warm room, not below 10°C (50°F); high humidity; bright light. **Care:** water only when becoming dry. **Propagation:** seeds early spring.

Beloperone guttata Shrimp plant
Habit: a small shrub, hardly ever out of flower. **Conditions:** warmth in summer, 10°C (50°F) during winter rest period; moderate humidity; bright light. **Care:** water well, far less when resting. **Propagation:** cuttings, spring.

Billbergia nutans Queen's tears
Habit: clump-forming evergreen perennial flowering regularly each year. **Conditions:** not below 10°C (50°F); high humidity; bright light. **Care:** keep steadily moist. Use small pots. **Propagation:** division, spring.

Blechnum gibbum
Habit: a dwarf evergreen fern. **Conditions:** ideal temperature 15.5°C (60°F) and above; high humidity; good light. **Care:** water well when growing, moderately in winter. **Propagation:** offsets in spring.

Bougainvillea 'Harrisii'   Variegated paper
flower
Habit: low bushy foliage plant.
Conditions: warmth in growing period, 7–
10°C (45–50°F) autumn/winter; plenty of sun;
moderate humidity. **Care:** moist in growing
period, in winter almost dry.
Propagation: cuttings, spring.

Bougainvillea spectabilis variety   Paper
flower
Habit: a climbing plant, flowering in
summer; various colours. **Conditions:** bright
light and sun; warmth in summer, 7–10°C
(45–50°F) autumn/winter; moderate
humidity. **Care:** keep dryish in winter; prune
early spring.

Caladium hortulanum 'Candidum'   Angel's
wings
Habit: a herbaceous perennial foliage plant.
Conditions: ideally above 21°C (70°F), not
below 15.5°C (60°F); very high humidity;
moderately bright light. **Care:** water well, but
dry off for the winter; store warm.

Calathea lancifolia
Habit: dwarf, slow, evergreen perennial.
Conditions: minimum temperature of 10°C
(50°F); very high humidity; suitable for light
shade. **Care:** keep steadily moist.
Propagation: division in spring.

Calathea makoyana Peacock plant
Habit: evergreen perennial to 60 cm (2 ft).
Conditions, care and propagation as for *C. lancifolia*. All calatheas benefit from liquid feeding in summer, and an eye should be kept open for aphids on young leaves.

Calathea ornata 'Sanderiana'
Habit: evergreen foliage perennial up to 1 m (3 ft) high. Like all calatheas, it comes from tropical rain forests, and needs the same care and conditions as *C. lancifolia*. High humidity is essential.

Calathea zebrina Zebra plant
Habit: this is one of the most striking of the calatheas, on account of its boldly striped leaves. It grows to a height of about 60 cm (2 ft). The leaves have a velvety texture.
Cultivation: as for *C. lancifolia*.

Calceolaria hybrid Slipper wort
Habit: a short-term pot plant which blooms in the spring. Various bright colours.
Conditions: cool, temperature of 10°C (50°F) is ideal; moderate humidity; bright light.
Care: keep steadily moist.
Propagation: seeds, spring.

Campanula isophylla 'Alba' Bellflower
Habit: a trailing perennial flowering in
summer and autumn. Also a blue form.
Conditions: grow in a cool room; slight
humidity, bright light. **Care:** keep barely
moist in winter. **Propagation:** cuttings.

Capsicum annuum Ornamental pepper
Habit: a short-term pot plant with winter
berries. **Conditions:** grow cool at all times;
dry air; good bright light. **Care:** keep steadily
moist. **Propagation:** plants can be raised from
seeds sown in spring.

Ceropegia woodii Rosary vine
Habit: trailing succulent plant.
Conditions: bright light, some sun; dry
atmosphere; minimum temperature of 10°C
(50°F). **Care:** water only as compost is drying
out, keep only just moist in winter.

Chamaecereus sylvestrii Peanut cactus
Habit: a dwarf spreading cactus which
flowers very freely. **Conditions:** cool in
winter – around 7–10°C (45–50°F); sunny
spot; dry air. **Care:** keep dry in autumn and
winter. **Propagation:** cuttings in summer.

Chamaedorea elegans (Neanthe bella)
Parlour palm
Habit: grows to about 1 m (3 ft).
Conditions: warm room, but cooler in
winter – around 10°C (50°F); suitable for light
shade; high humidity. **Care:** keep compost
only slightly moist all year round.

Chamaerops humilis European fan palm
Habit: about 1 m (3 ft) high when pot grown.
Conditions and care as for *Chamaedorea
elegans*. Palms must have good drainage and
should only be potted on when they are
completely pot-bound.

Chlorophytum comosum 'Variegatum'
Spider plant
Habit: perennial evergreen foliage plant.
Conditions: very adaptable; minimum
temperature of 7°C (45°F); high humidity
when warm; bright light or shade.
Care: water well in growing season.
Propagation: division.

Chrysanthemum Dwarf pot
chrysanthemum
Habit: short-term pot plant, available all year
round. Wide range of colours.
Conditions: keep in cool room; bright light,
dryish air. **Care:** keep steadily moist at all
times. Discard after flowering.

Cissus antarctica Kangaroo vine
Habit: a climbing evergreen.
Conditions: minimum temperature of 4.5°C
(40°F), but ideally warm room; moderate
humidity; bright light to shade.
Care: compost should almost dry out
between waterings. **Propagation:** cuttings.

Cissus rhombifolia 'Ellen Danica' Grape
ivy
Habit: evergreen climber.
Conditions: minimum temperature of 4.5°C
(40°F); moderate humidity; bright light to
deep shade. **Care:** allow to almost dry out
between waterings. **Propagation:** cuttings,
spring.

Citrus microcarpa (C. mitis) Calamondin or
dwarf orange
Habit: 45 cm (18 in) high, fragrant flowers.
Conditions: minimum temperature of 13°C
(55°F); bright light; humid air. **Care:** water
sparingly in winter; feed monthly in
summer; light pruning late winter.

Clerodendrum thomsoniae Glory bower
Habit: a climber flowering in summer.
Conditions: minimum temperature of 13°C
(55°F); warm in summer; bright light; humid
air. **Care:** water sparingly in autumn/winter.
Prune late winter. **Propagation:** spring
cuttings.

Clivia miniata   Kaffir lily
Habit: a perennial, flowering in spring.
Conditions: 10°C (50°F) winter, 15.5°C (60°F)
summer; a little humidity; sunny spot.
Care: water well spring/summer, barely
moist in winter. Pot on only when pot-
bound.

Codiaeum variegatum 'Pictum'   Croton
Habit: evergreen foliage shrub to about 1.2 m
(4 ft). **Conditions:** 21°C (70°F), not below
15.5°C (60°F); very high humidity; bright
light. **Care:** allow to almost dry out in winter,
water well in summer. Avoid draughts.

Coleus blumei   Flame nettle
Habit: short-term foliage pot plant. Various
bright colours. **Conditions:** temperature of
about 15.5°C (60°F); humid air; bright light.
Care: keep moist at all times.
Propagation: seeds, sown in the spring.

Cordyline indivisa   Cabbage tree
Habit: an evergreen shrub to about 1.5 m
(5 ft). **Conditions:** suitable for a cool room
(hardy in some areas); slight humidity;
bright light. **Care:** be sparing with water in
the autumn/winter.

Cordyline terminalis Cabbage palm
Habit: height to about 1 m (3 ft), several
varieties, leaves various colours.
Conditions: 21°C (70°F) by day, 13–15.5°C (55–
60°F) at night; high humidity; bright light.
Care: water sparingly autumn/winter.

Crassula falcata
Habit: dwarf succulent plant.
Conditions: cool in winter – 10°C (50°F),
warm in summer; sunshine essential; dry air
needed. **Care:** water normally, but keep dry
in autumn/winter. **Propagation:** summer
cuttings.

Crassula portulacea Jade tree
Habit: a branching succulent, very easy to
grow. **Conditions,** care and propagation as
for *C. falcata*. As with all succulents, at all
costs avoid keeping the compost very wet or
roots may rot.

Crossandra infundibuliformis Firecracker
flower
Habit: a tropical shrub flowering in spring
and summer. **Conditions:** warmth needed,
never below 13°C (55°F); diffused light; high
humidity. **Care:** allow to partially dry out
between waterings. **Propagation:** cuttings.

Cryptanthus bivittatus Earth star
Habit: a low-growing bromeliad.
Conditions: 15.5°C (60°F) and above,
minimum of 10°C (50°F); high humidity;
bright light. Keep moist all year round; pot
on only when pot-bound and use small pots.
Propagation: offsets.

Cryptanthus zonatus Earth star
Habit: low-growing bromeliad, one of the
most striking species. Conditions, care and
propagation as for *C. bivittatus*. The
cryptanthus are ideal plants for growing in
glass cases or fish tanks.

Ctenanthe oppenheimiana 'Tricolor'
Habit: a 60–90 cm (2–3 ft) high evergreen
perennial. **Conditions:** minimum
temperature 15.5°C (60°F); high humidity;
suitable for light shade. **Care:** keep compost
steadily moist, reduce watering in winter.
Propagation: division.

Cuphea ignea Cigar plant
Habit: a small summer-flowering shrubby
plant. **Conditions:** minimum temperature 7°C
(45°F); bright light, plus some sun; dryish air.
Care: keep steadily moist. **Propagation:** raise
new plants annually, spring cuttings.

Cycas revoluta Sago palm
Habit: slow-growing palm-like tree.
Conditions: warm room, but cool in winter –
10°C (50°F); humidity; light shade. **Care:** keep
only slightly moist in winter, water more
freely in summer. Pot on when pot-bound.

Cyclamen persicum
Habit: tuberous perennial, autumn/winter
flowering. **Conditions:** temperature 13–15.5°C
(55–60°F); moderate humidity; bright light.
Care: water only when becoming dry. Keep
dry from late spring to late summer to rest
the plants.

Cyperus alternifolius Umbrella plant
Habit: a small foliage perennial.
Conditions: temperature 15.5°C (60°F),
minimum of 10°C (50°F); high humidity;
bright light, or slight shade. **Care:** keep
compost wet all year round.
Propagation: division, spring.

Cyrtomium falcatum Holly fern
Habit: fronds (leaves) up to 60 cm (2 ft) long.
Conditions: temperature range 10–15.5°C (50–
60°F); only slight humidity; bright light or
slight shade. **Care:** water sparingly in low
temperatures. **Propagation:** division.

Cytisus × racemosus
Habit: a small spring-flowering shrub.
Conditions: cool room, minimum of 4.5°C
(40°F); place outdoors in summer; bright
light; humidity in warm conditions.
Care: water sparingly in winter.
Propagation: cuttings.

Dieffenbachia maculata Dumb cane
Habit: large shrubby plant, evergreen foliage.
Conditions: 21°C (70°F), minimum of 15.5°C
(60°F); high humidity; bright light.
Care: keep steadily moist throughout year.
Propagation: cuttings of stem sections.

Dionaea muscipula Venus fly trap
Habit: dwarf carnivorous plant – 'jaws' snap
together trapping flies.
Conditions: minimum winter temperature of
4.5°C (40°F); high humidity in summer;
bright light. **Care:** keep wet in spring/
summer, only just moist autumn/winter.

Dizygotheca elegantissima False aralia
Habit: a shrubby plant growing slowly to
about 1.2 m (4 ft) in height.
Conditions: temperature 15.5°C (60°F), not
below 13°C (55°F); high humidity; bright
light. **Care:** keep only slightly moist.
Propagation: cuttings.

Dracaena deremensis 'Warneckii'
Habit: palm-like shrub, ideal specimen plant.
Conditions: ideal temperature 21°C (70°F),
not below 13°C (55°F); very high humidity;
bright light. **Care:** water well, far less in
winter. **Propagation:** cuttings.

Dracaena fragrans 'Massangeana'
Habit: a palm-like specimen shrub.
Conditions, care and propagation as for
D. deremensis 'Warneckii'. Like most
dracaenas it is quite a rapid grower and soon
makes a substantial specimen.

Dracaena marginata
Habit: this has a palm-like stem and grows to
about 1.2 m (4 ft) in height. Even more
attractive is the cream and pink variegated
'Tricolor'. Easy and very tough, standing
lower temperatures than other dracaenas.

Dracaena surculosa (D. godseffiana)
Habit: 60 cm (2 ft) tall, with a bushy habit of
growth. There are varieties with even more
colourful leaves, such as 'Florida Beauty' and
'Kelleri'. Conditions and care as for the other
dracaenas.

Epiphyllum hybrid Orchid cactus
Habit: an epiphytic or tree-dwelling cactus which flowers profusely in summer. Many hybrids in various colours. **Conditions:** 10°C (50°F), in winter; high humidity, summer; bright light. **Care:** keep moist all year round.

Erica gracilis Cape heath
Habit: small shrub, winter flowering. **Conditions:** must be kept in cool room – 4.5–13°C (40–55°F); bright light plus some sun; humid air. **Care:** keep steadily moist. Prune after flowering. Stand outside in summer.

Euphorbia millii Crown of thorns
Habit: a succulent shrub flowering in winter and spring. **Conditions:** minimum winter temperature of 10°C (50°F); dry atmosphere; maximum light, plus some sun. **Care:** water occasionally in winter, normally in summer.

Euphorbia pulcherrima Poinsettia
Habit: shrubby plant flowering at Christmas time. Generally discarded after flowering. **Conditions:** temperature of 15.5°C (60°F); slight humidity; maximum light. **Care:** allow compost to partially dry out between waterings.

Exacum affine Persian violet
Habit: a dwarf bushy plant flowering
summer and autumn, discarded afterwards.
Conditions: ideal temperature around 15.5°C
(60°F); maximum light; humidity. **Care:** keep
steadily moist. **Propagation:** seeds in spring.

× **Fatshedera lizei**
Habit: a climber with evergreen foliage.
Conditions: ideal plant for cool room;
moderate humidity; slight shade. **Care:** water
well in summer, less in winter. Can prune
back late winter. **Propagation:** cuttings.

Fatsia japonica Japanese aralia
Habit: a hardy evergreen foliage shrub.
Conditions: ideal for unheated or cool room;
dry air; shade or bright light. **Care:** water
well in summer, but sparingly in winter.
Propagation: summer cuttings.

Ficus benjamina Weeping fig
Habit: a small tree about 2 m (6 ft) high. Ideal
specimen plant. **Conditions:** temperature
range of 15.5–21°C (60–70°F); high humidity;
bright light to slight shade. **Care:** keep
compost on dry side in winter.

Ficus deltoidea Mistletoe fig
Habit: a shrub to 60 cm (2 ft) in height, bearing yellow berries. Makes an interesting and unusual specimen plant. Conditions and care as for *F. benjamina*. **Propagation:** stem cuttings, summer.

Ficus elastica 'Decora' Rubber plant
Habit: evergreen tree, popularly used as a specimen plant. Conditions and care as for *F. benjamina*. If the plant becomes too tall the top can be cut out in the spring, when the plant will branch.

Ficus elastica 'Schryveriana' Rubber plant
Habit: one of the several variegated forms of rubber plant, same habit as *elastica*. Conditions and care as for *F. benjamina*, although you should ensure bright light for the best leaf colour.

Ficus lyrata Fiddle-back fig
Habit: a vigorous tree soon attaining a height of 2 m (6 ft) plus. Massive leaves. Conditions and care as for *F. benjamina*. As with *elastica*, the top can be cut out if the plant becomes too tall.

Ficus pumila Creeping fig
Habit: a trailing or climbing plant of modest growth. Useful for the edges of groups or for hanging containers. Conditions and care as for *F. benjamina*. **Propagation:** stem cuttings in summer.

Fittonia verschaffeltii Mosaic plant
Habit: low-growing, creeping foliage perennial. **Conditions:** temperature between 15.5 and 21°C (60 and 70°F); very high humidity; light shade. **Care:** keep only slightly moist. **Propagation:** cuttings in spring.

Gardenia jasminoides Cape jasmine
Habit: a shrub with highly fragrant blooms in spring. **Conditions:** warmth needed, not below 15.5°C (60°F); bright light; high humidity. **Care:** keep steadily moist. Avoid fluctuating temperatures.

Gasteria verrucosa Cape hart's tongue
Habit: low-growing succulent plant.
Conditions: keep cool in winter – around 7–10°C (45–50°F); sunny spot; dry air.
Care: water normally spring/summer; keep dry in autumn/winter. **Propagation:** leaf cuttings.

Glechoma hederacea 'Variegata' (Nepeta hederacea 'Variegata') Ground ivy
Habit: a trailing perennial, ideal for hanging baskets. **Conditions:** a hardy plant, suitable for cool or cold rooms; dry air; bright light. **Care:** water sparingly in winter.

Grevillea robusta Silk oak
Habit: a quick-growing tree, soon attaining 2 m (6 ft) in height. **Conditions:** temperature 13–18°C (55–65°F); moderate humidity; bright light, or slight shade. **Care:** water very sparingly in winter. **Propagation:** seeds.

Guzmania lingulata
Habit: one of the bromeliads, an evergreen perennial. **Conditions:** minimum temperature 10°C (50°F); high humidity when warm; bright light. **Care:** keep moist throughout year. Keep 'vase' filled with fresh water.

Guzmania lingulata minor
Habit: a slightly smaller plant than *G. lingulata*, but needing exactly the same conditions. When buying any guzmania ensure that the plant has a flower stem, or is actually in flower. **Propagation:** division.

Gymnocalycium species Chin cactus
Habit: small, globular, free-flowering cactus.
Conditions: in winter provide 4.5°C (40°F),
warmth in summer; sunny position; dry air.
Care: keep compost dry in autumn/winter,
water normally in growing season.

Gynura aurantiaca Velvet plant
Habit: a spreading evergreen perennial.
Conditions: warm room, minimum
temperature 10°C (50°F); moderate humidity
or dry air; bright light. **Care:** water well in
growing season. **Propagation:** cuttings,
spring.

Hedera helix variety Common ivy
Habit: an upright-growing form of the
common ivy. **Conditions:** a hardy plant, ideal
for cold or cool room; slight humidity;
suitable for shade. **Care:** water only as
compost is drying out. **Propagation:** cuttings.

Hedera helix variety Variegated common
ivy
Habit: one of the many varieties of
variegated ivy, with a trailing or climbing
habit of growth. Care and conditions as
described. However, the variegated ivies
need more light or the colour may fade.

Hedera canariensis 'Variegata' Variegated Canary Island ivy
Habit: a popular and vigorous large-leaved ivy – use as a trailer or climber. Care and conditions as described, but provide good light for best leaf colour, although it will thrive in shade.

Hibiscus rosa-sinensis 'Cooperi' Variegated rose of China
Habit: a shrubby plant grown for its variegated foliage. **Conditions:** minimum temperature 13°C (55°F); sunny spot; moderate humidity. **Care:** water very sparingly in winter, well in summer. **Propagation:** cuttings.

Hibiscus rosa-sinensis hybrid Rose of China
Habit: shrubby plant; there are now many hybrids in various brilliant colours. All need the same conditions and care as 'Cooperi'. Established plants are best pruned hard in late winter.

Hippeastrum hybrid
Habit: a bulb which flowers in spring or summer. **Conditions:** keep cool in winter, more warmth in summer; dryish atmosphere; maximum light. **Care:** keep compost dry over winter to give plant a rest.

Howea belmoreana Palm
Habit: slow grower, eventually reaching
about 2.4 m (8 ft). **Conditions:** warm room,
not below 13°C (55°F); bright light or shade;
humid atmosphere. **Care:** keep steadily moist
throughout the year. Pot on when pot-
bound.

Hoya bella Wax flower
Habit: a dwarf shrub of spreading habit,
flowering in summer. **Conditions:** provide
winter temperature of 10°C (50°F); high
humidity in warm conditions; bright light,
plus some sun. **Care:** water very sparingly in
winter.

Hydrangea macrophylla Florists' hydrangea
Habit: deciduous shrub flowering in spring
or summer. Treated as short-term pot plant.
Conditions: for cool room; provide
humidity; bright light or slight shade.
Care: plenty of water needed when in full
growth.

Hypocyrta glabra Clog plant
Habit: a bushy free-flowering plant,
blooming in spring and summer.
Conditions: minimum temperature of 10°C
(50°F); bright light or slight shade; humid air.
Care: water very sparingly in winter.
Propagation: cuttings.

Hypoestes sanguinolenta   Polka dot plant
Habit: dwarf bushy foliage plant, best raised from seeds each year. **Conditions:** provide temperature range of 13–18°C (55–65°F); high humidity; bright light. **Care:** avoid very wet compost. **Propagation:** seeds, spring.

Impatiens walleriana   Busy lizzie
Habit: a free-flowering perennial, discarded after flowering. **Conditions:** temperature range 13–21°C (55–70°F); high humidity; bright light. **Care:** water copiously, remove dead flowers. **Propagation:** seeds, spring.

Iresine herbstii variety
Habit: small foliage plant, best raised from cuttings each year. **Conditions:** minimum temperature of 13°C (55°F); sunny position; high humidity. **Care:** keep moist at all times. **Propagation:** cuttings, spring.

Jacaranda mimosifolia
Habit: a tree, grown for its ferny foliage. **Conditions:** minimum temperature of 13°C (55°F); bright light, some sun; humid air. **Care:** moderate watering, keep dryish in winter. **Propagation:** seeds in spring.

Kalanchoe blossfeldiana hybrid
Habit: a succulent which blooms in winter or spring. **Conditions:** minimum temperature of 10°C (50°F); maximum light; dry air. **Care:** allow to partially dry out between waterings. **Propagation:** cuttings in summer.

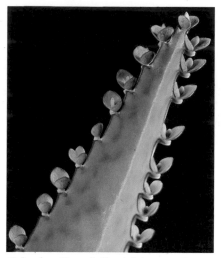

Kalanchoe (Bryophyllum) daigremontianum
Habit: a tall succulent plant, producing plantlets on leaf edges.
Conditions: minimum temperature of 10°C (50°F); sunny spot; dry air. **Care:** keep dry in winter, moderate watering in summer.
Propagation: pot plantlets.

Mammillaria prolifera texana
Habit: a vigorous, free-flowering, clump-forming cactus. **Conditions:** winter temperature of about 7°C (45°F); sunny position; dry air. **Care:** keep dry in autumn/winter. **Propagation:** remove offsets.

Mammillaria sheldonii
Habit: a slightly taller species, and quite choice, but available from cactus growers. It has larger flowers than many species. Like all mammillarias it needs a gritty compost. Cultivation, etc., as for *M. prolifera.*

Maranta leuconeura 'Fascinator' Prayer plant
Habit: a low-growing evergreen foliage perennial. **Conditions:** 15.5–21°C (60–70°F), not below 10°C (50°F); high humidity; bright light. **Care:** keep steadily moist. **Propagation:** cuttings or division in spring.

Maranta leuconeura 'Kerchoveana' Prayer plant
Habit: also a low-growing perennial grown for its attractive foliage. Like all marantas, the leaves move into a vertical position during darkness. Conditions, care and propagation as for *M.l.* 'Fascinator'.

Mimosa pudica Sensitive plant
Habit: a shrub which is normally grown as an annual. Rapidly folds its leaves when touched. **Conditions:** minimum of 15.5°C (60°F); sunny spot; humid air. **Care:** keep steadily moist. **Propagation:** seeds, spring.

Monstera deliciosa Swiss cheese plant
Habit: a climber, making a superb specimen plant. **Conditions:** 15.5–21°C (60–70°F), not below 10°C (50°F); high humidity; slight shade. **Care:** keep only just moist in winter. **Propagation:** sections of stem as cuttings.

Neoregelia carolinae 'Tricolor'
Habit: one of the 'vase-forming' bromeliads, an evergreen perennial. **Conditions:** plenty of warmth in summer, minimum of 10°C (50°F) in winter; high humidity; good light. **Care:** keep steadily moist, and vase filled with fresh water.

Nephrolepis exaltata variety   Sword fern
Habit: perennial foliage plant, arching habit of growth. **Conditions:** steady temperature of 15.5°C (60°F) is ideal; high humidity; bright light. **Care:** keep compost steadily moist. **Propagation:** division.

Nerium oleander   Oleander
Habit: a fairly large shrub flowering summer and autumn. **Conditions:** minimum winter temperature of 7°C (45°C); sunny position; takes dryish air. **Care:** water sparingly in winter. Cut back flowered stems in autumn.

Nertera granadensis   Bead plant'
Habit: a low creeping plant producing its berries in autumn. **Conditions:** grow in a cool room; sunny spot; dry air. **Care:** water sparingly during winter. Place outdoors in summer. **Propagation:** division, spring.

Notocactus ottonis
Habit: a free-flowering cactus.
Conditions: winter temperature of about 7°C
(45°F); sunny position; dry air. **Care:** keep
dry in autumn/winter. **Propagation:** remove
and pot up offsets in the spring.

Pachystachys lutea Lollipop plant
Habit: a small shrubby plant flowering in
summer and autumn. **Conditions:** minimum
winter temperature of 13°C (55°F); maximum
light; humid air. **Care:** water sparingly in
winter; prune in spring.
Propagation: cuttings.

Pedilanthus tithymaloides 'Variegata'
Habit: a shrubby succulent about 60 cm (2 ft)
high. **Conditions:** minimum temperature of
10°C (50°F) in winter; bright light; dry
atmosphere. **Care:** hardly any watering
needed in winter rest period.
Propagation: cuttings.

Pelargonium graveolens 'Variegatum'
Geranium
Habit: a bushy perennial grown for its
foliage. **Conditions:** minimum winter
temperature 7°C (45°F); sunny spot; dry air.
Care: water sparingly in autumn/winter.
Propagation: cuttings in late summer.

Pellaea rotundifolia Button fern
Habit: a small prostrate fern.
Conditions: minimum winter temperature of 10°C (50°F); humid air; best in light shade.
Care: keep steadily moist. Pot on when pot-bound. **Propagation:** division in spring.

Peperomia argyreia Pepper elder
Habit: a low-growing evergreen foliage perennial. **Conditions:** warm room, not below 13°C (55°F); high humidity; slight shade or bright light. **Care:** allow compost to almost dry out before watering.
Propagation: division.

Peperomia caperata Pepper elder
Habit: very popular species, about 15 cm (6 in) high. Conditions, care and propagation as for *P. argyreia*. Peperomias are especially good subjects for growing in bottle gardens or fish tanks.

Philodendron erubescens
Habit: a climbing evergreen; use as a specimen plant. **Conditions:** try to provide 21°C (70°F), not below 15.5°C (60°F); high humidity; ideal for shade. **Care:** water well in summer, moderately in winter.
Propagation: cuttings.

Philodendron laciniatum
Habit: a slow-growing climbing species up to 1.2 m (4 ft) high. Conditions, care and propagation as for *P. erubescens*. Like all climbing species, it can be grown up a moss pole for support.

Philodendron scandens
Habit: this species is popular and can be grown as a climber or as a trailing plant. It has much smaller leaves than most other philodendrons. Conditions, care and propagation as for *P. erubescens*.

Philodendron selloum
Habit: this is a vigorous, fast-growing species of non-climbing habit. It is very space-consuming – each leaf can be up to 38 cm (15 in) across. Conditions, care and propagation as for *P. erubescens*.

Phoenix roebelenii Pygmy date palm
Habit: when young it has a low spreading shape. **Conditions:** provide a minimum temperature of 15.5°C (60°F); bright light, or slight shade; humid air. **Care:** water only when almost dry in winter. Pot on when pot-bound.

Pilea cadierei Aluminium plant
Habit: low-growing evergreen perennial grown for its foliage. **Conditions:** 15.5°C (60°F), not below 13°C (55°C); moderate humidity; slight shade. **Care:** water only when compost has almost dried out. **Propagation:** cuttings.

Pilea microphylla Artillery plant
Habit: a dwarf bushy evergreen perennial with very tiny leaves. Conditions, care and propagation as for *P. cadierei*. Raise new plants regularly as older plants are not so attractive. Cuttings root easily.

Primula obconica
Habit: a short-term pot plant which flowers in winter or spring. **Conditions:** cool room, not above 15.5°C (60°F); moderate humidity; maximum light. **Care:** keep the compost steadily moist. **Propagation:** seeds, in spring.

Pteris cretica 'Albolineata' Ribbon fern
Habit: a popular fern, growing to about 45 cm (18 in) high. **Conditions:** temperature ideally not below 15.5°C (60°F); high humidity; bright light. **Care:** keep steadily moist; pot on when pot-bound. **Propagation:** division.

Rhododendron simsii Azalea
Habit: a low-growing evergreen shrub flowering in winter and spring. Various colours available. **Conditions:** keep cool – not above 15.5°C (60°F); humid air; bright light. **Care:** do not allow to dry out; use rainwater.

Rhoeo spathacea 'Vittata' Moses in the cradle
Habit: evergreen perennial, low spreading habit. **Conditions:** provide a temperature of 15.5–21°C (60–70°F); high humidity; light to deep shade. **Care:** water very sparingly in winter. **Propagation:** cuttings, spring.

Rochea coccinea
Habit: a small bushy succulent flowering in spring or summer. **Conditions:** keep at about 7°C (45°F) in winter: sunny spot; dry air. **Care:** keep only slightly moist in winter; prune back after flowering. **Propagation:** cuttings.

Saintpaulia ionantha African violet
Habit: rosette-forming perennial with long flowering period. Many colours available. **Conditions:** needs a temperature of 15.5–18°C (60–65°F); high humidity; bright light. **Care:** only needs small pot; keep drier in winter.

Sansevieria trifasciata 'Laurentii' Mother-in-law's tongue
Habit: a popular perennial plant, about 1 m (3 ft) high. **Conditions:** temperature ideally 15.5–21°C (60–70°F), minimum of 10°C (50°F); dry atmosphere; bright sun or shade. **Care:** water only when compost drying out.

Saxifraga stolonifera 'Tricolor' Mother of thousands
Habit: evergreen perennial producing plantlets on long stems. **Conditions:** grow in cool room; humid air in warm weather; bright light. **Care:** water only when dry in winter. **Propagation:** pot plantlets.

Schefflera actinophylla Umbrella tree
Habit: a small well-branched tree, about 2 m (6 ft) tall. **Conditions:** minimum winter temperature 13°C (55°F); high humidity; bright light. **Care:** allow compost to almost dry out in winter before watering.

Schlumbergera hybrid Christmas cactus
Habit: flowers at Christmas time. Various colours. **Conditions:** minimum winter temperature of 10°C (50°F); high humidity in warm conditions; bright light. **Care:** keep moist all year round. **Propagation:** cuttings.

Scindapsus aureus Devil's ivy
Habit: evergreen climber; can be grown as a trailer. **Conditions:** temperature ideally 21°C (70°F), not below 15.5°C (60°F); high humidity; bright light or shade.
Care: slightly moist. **Propagation:** cuttings in spring.

Scindapsus pictus 'Argyraeus' Devil's ivy
Habit: a climber, which can also be allowed to trail. **Conditions:** ideally 21°C (70°F), not below 15.5°C (60°F); high humidity; bright light to deep shade. **Care:** keep only slightly moist in winter. **Propagation:** cuttings.

Sedum morganianum Stonecrop
Habit: a succulent with 60 cm (2 ft) long trailing stems. **Conditions:** keep at about 7–10°C (45–50°F) in winter; maximum light, plus some sun; dry air. **Care:** keep dry in winter. **Propagation:** cuttings, summer.

Senecio × hybridus Cineraria
Habit: a short-term pot plant flowering in winter and spring. **Conditions:** keep cool – not above 15.5°C (60°F); moderate humidity; maximum light. **Care:** keep steadily moist. **Propagation:** seeds, sown in spring.

Setcreasea purpurea   Purple heart
Habit: a trailing foliage perennial.
Conditions: minimum temperature of 10°C
(50°F); bright light; humid air. **Care:** water
well when growing, sparingly in winter.
Propagation: cuttings spring or summer.

Sinningia speciosa   Gloxinia
Habit: summer-flowering pot plant, many
colours, which grows from a tuber.
Conditions: minimum of 15.5°C (60°F); high
humidity; bright light. **Care:** pot tuber in
spring, dry off for winter rest.

Solanum pseudocapsicum   Winter cherry
Habit: dwarf shrubby plant with winter
berries. Discard after fruiting.
Conditions: keep cool – around 10°C (50°F);
moderate humidity; bright light. **Care:** keep
steadily moist. **Propagation:** seeds in spring.

Soleirolia (Helxine) soleirolii   Mind-your-
own-business
Habit: a carpeting, spreading perennial
grown for its foliage. **Conditions:** for cool
room, not below 7°C (45°F); shade to bright
light; humidity in warm conditions.
Care: keep moist. **Propagation:** division.

Spathiphyllum wallisii White sails
Habit: an evergreen perennial flowering in
spring or summer. **Conditions:** ideally 15.5°C
(60°F), not below 13°C (55°F); high humidity;
bright light. **Care:** keep only just moist in
winter. **Propagation:** division in spring.

Stephanotis floribunda Madagascar jasmine
Habit: a vigorous climber with heavily
scented flowers summer and autumn.
Conditions: warmth, not below 13°C (55°F) in
winter; bright light; humidity. **Care:** keep
steadily moist. Prune after flowering.

Streptocarpus hybrid Cape primrose
Habit: low-growing perennial flowering in
summer. Various colours. **Conditions:** ideal
temperature 15.5–18°C (60–65°F), but 10°C
(50°F) during winter; moderate humidity;
bright light. **Care:** keep dryish in winter.

Syngonium podophyllum Goose foot
Habit: a small climbing evergreen perennial.
Grow also as trailer. **Conditions:** 21°C (70°F)
ideal, not below 15.5°C (60°F); moderate
humidity; slight shade or bright light.
Care: keep steadily moist throughout year.

Syngonium podophyllum 'Green Gold'
Goose foot
Habit: as species, but more attractive foliage.
Conditions and care as for the species.
Propagation: syngoniums are raised from
cuttings in the spring or summer and root
quite easily.

Tillandsia flabellata
Habit: a rosette-forming bromeliad of modest
size. **Conditions:** minimum winter
temperature of 10°c (50°F); high humidity,
bright light. **Care:** keep steadily moist all
year round. **Propagation:** division.

Tillandsia ionantha   Air plant
Habit: a small epiphytic (tree-dwelling)
bromeliad. **Conditions:** must be grown on
piece of wood; not below 10°c (50°F); high
humidity; bright light. **Care:** mist spray plant
daily in warm conditions, weekly when cool.

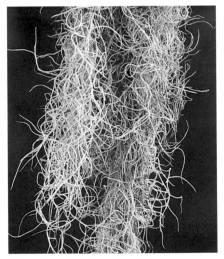

Tillandsia usneoides   Spanish moss
Habit: another epiphytic bromeliad
consisting of thread-like stems. Grow in the
same way as *T. ionantha.* Best hung up. Spray
the tillandsias only with rainwater or soft tap
water. **Propagation:** division.

Tolmiea menziesii Pick-a-back plant
Habit: evergreen perennial producing plantlets on leaves. **Conditions:** for cool or unheated room; slight humidity in warm weather; slight shade. **Care:** water moderately all year round. **Propagation:** pot plantlets.

Tradescantia blossfeldiana 'Variegata'
Wandering Jew
Habit: popular trailing perennial, evergreen. **Conditions:** not below 10°c (50°f); high humidity in warm conditions; bright light. **Care:** keep only just moist in winter. **Propagation:** cuttings spring or summer.

Vriesia splendens Flaming sword
Habit: a vase-forming bromeliad of modest size. **Conditions:** minimum winter temperature of 10°c (50°f); high humidity; bright light. **Care:** keep steadily moist all year round. **Propagation:** detach offsets.

Zebrina pendula 'Quadricolor' Wandering Jew
Habit: a popular evergreen trailing plant. **Conditions:** not below 10°c (50°f); high humidity in warm conditions; bright light. **Care:** keep only just moist in winter. **Propagation:** cuttings in spring or summer.

PLANTS FOR SPECIAL PURPOSES

Shady conditions

Aglaonema
Araucaria
Asparagus
Aspidistra
Asplenium bulbiferum
Begonia boweri
B. masoniana
B. rex
Calathea
Chamaedorea
Chamaerops
Chlorophytum
Cissus
Ctenanthe
Cycas
Cyperus
Cyrtomium
× Fatshedera
Fatsia
Ficus
Fittonia
Grevillea
Hedera
Howea
Hydrangea
Hypocyrta
Monstera

Pellaea
Peperomia
Philodendron
Phoenix
Pilea
Rhoeo
Sansevieria
Scindapsus
Soleirolia
Syngonium
Tolmiea

Sunny conditions

Aeonium
Agave
Aloe
Amaryllis
Aporocactus
Bougainvillea
Ceropegia
Chamaecereus
Clivia
Crassula
Cuphea
Erica
Euphorbia millii
Gasteria
Gymnocalycium

Hibiscus
Jacaranda
Mammillaria
Mimosa
Nerium
Nertera
Notocactus
Pelargonium
Rochea
Sansevieria
Sedum

Dry air

Aeonium
Agave
Aloe
Amaryllis
Aporocactus
Capsicum
Ceropegia
Chamaecereus
Chrysanthemum
Crassula
Cuphea
Euphorbia millii
Fatsia
Gasteria
Glechoma
Gymnocalycium

Hippeastrum
Kalanchoe
Mammillaria
Nerium
Nertera
Notocactus
Pedilanthus
Pelargonium
Rochea
Sansevieria
Sedum

Humid atmosphere

Achimenes
Adiantum
Aechmea
Aglaonema
Ananus
Anthurium
Aphelandra
Araucaria
Ardisia
Asparagus
Aspidistra
Asplenium
Begonia
Beloperone
Billbergia
Blechnum
Bougainvillea
Caladium
Calathea
Calceolaria
Campanula
Chamaedorea
Chamaerops
Chlorophytum
Cissus
Citrus
Clerodendrum
Clivia
Codiaeum

Coleus
Cordyline
Crossandra
Cryptanthus
Ctenanthe
Cycas
Cyclamen
Cyperus
Cyrtomium
Cytisus
Dieffenbachia
Dionaea
Dizygotheca
Dracaena
Epiphyllum
Erica
Euphorbia pulcherrima
Exacum
× Fatshedera
Ficus
Fittonia
Gardenia
Grevillea
Guzmania
Gynura
Hedera
Hibiscus
Howea
Hoya
Hydrangea
Hypocyrta
Hypoestes
Impatiens
Iresine
Jacaranda
Maranta
Mimosa
Monstera
Neoregelia
Nephrolepis
Pachystachys
Pellaea
Peperomia
Philodendron

Phoenix
Pilea
Primula
Pteris
Rhododendron
Rhoeo
Saintpaulia
Saxifraga
Schefflera
Schlumbergera
Scindapsus
Senecio
Setcreasea
Sinningia
Solanum
Soleirolia
Spathiphyllum
Stephanotis
Streptocarpus
Syngonium
Tillandsia
Tolmiea
Tradescantia
Vriesia
Zebrina

Cool rooms

Amaryllis
Ardisia
Calceolaria
Campanula
Capsicum
Chrysanthemum
Cuphea
Cytisus
Erica
× Fatshedera
Fatsia
Glechoma
Hedera
Hydrangea
Nertera
Primula

Rhododendron
Senecio
Soleirolia
Tolmiea

Tolerant of neglect

Aeonium
Agave
Aloe
Aporocactus
Aspidistra
Ceropegia
Chamaecereus
Chlorophytum
Cissus

Crassula
Euphorbia millii
Gasteria
Glechoma
Gymnocalycium
Kalanchoe
Mammillaria
Notocactus
Rochea
Sansevieria
Sedum

COMMON NAME INDEX